Prologue: "Footprints in the Sand: A Prelude to Success"

In a world where selling sand on a beach seems like a folly, enter Jake Sanderson, a whimsical entrepreneur with a pocket full of dreams and a heart full of determination. This is not just a story about grains of sand; it is a journey through the shifting landscapes of commerce, where success is sculpted one grain at a time.

Imagine a vast expanse of shoreline, where the horizon kisses the sea, and the sand stretches as far as the eye can see. It is here that Jake unfolds his tale, leaving footprints in the sand that mark not just a passage but a narrative of creative salesmanship.

As the sun rises and sets, so too do the tides of the market. In this prologue, we dip our toes into the ocean of possibilities, where each wave carries with it the potential for success or the undertow of challenges. Join us on the shore as we embark on a journey with Jake, exploring the fine art of selling, where every grain of sand holds a secret, and every tide brings a new opportunity.

So, dear reader, as we step into the sand-laden pages of this whimsical adventure, let the gentle lapping of waves be our guide. The story begins, footprints are laid, and the stage is set for a dance with destiny.

Keith Kirby
Author of "*How to: Sell Sand on a Beach*!"

Sand, Sales, and Seashores

Not so long ago, on a sun-kissed beach where the golden sand stretched for miles, there stood a peculiar figure amid the colourful umbrellas and the laughter of beachgoers. Dressed in a crisp suit despite the scorching sun, Jake Sanderson saw an opportunity where others saw only grains beneath their toes.

With a charismatic smile, Jake set up a small stand adorned with signs that proclaimed, "The Best Sand on the Beach!" Curious sunbathers and families began to gather around, eyeing the salesperson with a mixture of scepticism and intrigue.

"What's so special about your sand?" a sceptical surfer asked, eyeing the vast expanse of beach surrounding them.

Jake, ever the salesperson, began his pitch. "Ladies and gentlemen, I present to you the most extraordinary sand you'll ever encounter. This is not your ordinary beach sand; this is a game-changer! Why settle for the mundane when you can have the extraordinary?"

He gestured to two separate piles of sand on his table—one seemingly wet, the other bone-dry. "Behold, the WetWonder and the DryDream! The WetWonder is perfect for building sandcastles that defy the relentless tide. No more watching your masterpieces wash away!"

A murmur of interest swept through the crowd. Jake continued, "And for those seeking pure relaxation, the DryDream is unparalleled. It is like a personal beach oasis—no need to worry about a grain sticking to your skin. It is the creme de la creme of beach experiences!"

As the crowd listened, captivated by Jake's enthusiasm, he went on to explain the innovative techniques behind his sand. "You see, our sand undergoes a patented treatment process that ensures it remains consistently damp or dry, depending on your preference. It's the result of years of research and development to give you the best beach experience possible."

To demonstrate the durability of his sandcastles, Jake sculpted intricate structures with the WetWonder. The crowd watched in amazement as the waves crashed against the shoreline, but the sandcastle stood defiant, a testament to the superior quality of Jake's product.

Word spread like wildfire along the beach, and soon, people were lining up to purchase Jake's extraordinary sand. Buckets of WetWonder and DryDream flew off the shelves, and families, children, and even curious seagulls revelled in the newfound beach luxury.

As the day wore on, Jake's once-sceptical customers became his biggest advocates. They built towering sandcastles, lounged on the DryDream with unparalleled comfort, and marvelled at the ingenious creation that had turned a free commodity into a hot-selling beachside sensation.

By sunset, Jake stood proudly beside his nearly empty stand, counting the proceeds of a day well spent. He had successfully sold sand on a beach, turning a seemingly impossible task into a triumph of marketing and innovation. As the last rays of the sun dipped below the horizon, Jake could not help but smile—proof that with the right pitch, even the most abundant resources could find their way into the hearts (and wallets) of those who dared to dream of something more extraordinary.

Synopsis

In the enchanting tale, "Sand, Sales, and Seashores," Jake Sanderson, a charismatic salesperson, transforms the mundane act of selling sand on a beach into a riveting adventure. Setting up shop on a bustling shoreline, Jake claims to possess the "Best Sand on the Beach" and captivates beachgoers with his promises of extraordinary experiences.

With an innovative approach, Jake introduces two distinct sands: the WetWonder, perfect for building sandcastles resistant to the relentless tide, and the DryDream, an oasis of comfort for those seeking relaxation. Through a blend of charisma and showmanship, Jake unveils the patented treatment process behind his sands, turning what is typically a free commodity into a must-have luxury.

As sceptical sunbathers become curious customers, Jake's pitch gains momentum. He displays the durability of his sandcastles, leaving the crowd in awe. Word quickly spreads along the beach, and soon, people are lining up to experience the WetWonder and DryDream for themselves.

Throughout the day, families, children, and even seagulls become avid fans of Jake's extraordinary sands. Buckets of WetWonder and DryDream fly off the shelves, and the once-sceptical customers become Jake's biggest advocates. By sunset, Jake stands proudly, having successfully turned a seemingly impossible task into a triumph of marketing and innovation.

"Sand, Sales, and Seashores" is a whimsical story that explores the power of marketing, innovation, and the unexpected value that can be found in the most commonplace things. It is a reminder that with the right pitch, even the most abundant resources can be transformed into coveted treasures, leaving readers with a smile and a newfound appreciation for the extraordinary in the ordinary.

Analysing Jake Sanderson's Sales Techniques in "Sand, Sales, and Seashores"

Jake Sanderson, the charismatic protagonist of our tale, employs a range of clever sales techniques to turn the seemingly impossible task of selling sand on a beach into a triumphant success. Let us delve into the key strategies he employed and how these can be applied to more practical products in real-world sales scenarios.

1. **Identifying Unique Selling Points (USPs):** Jake clearly understands the importance of differentiation. By presenting two distinct sands, the WetWonder and the DryDream, he creates a clear narrative around unique selling points. This strategy can be applied to any product or service by identifying and highlighting features that set it apart from competitors. Finding a niche or creating unique variations can capture customer attention and set the foundation for successful sales.

2. **Compelling Storytelling:** Jake's ability to weave a captivating story about the development and benefits of his sand engages the audience. Storytelling humanizes the product, making it relatable and memorable. In practical sales, the art of storytelling can be employed to create emotional connections with customers, making them more likely to remember and choose a product based on the narrative surrounding it.

3. **Demonstration and Showmanship:** The live demonstration of building sandcastles with the WetWonder serves as a powerful visual aid, displaying the product's quality and durability. In real-world sales, product demonstrations or interactive experiences can be powerful tools to give customers a firsthand taste of the product's benefits. This tactile approach helps in building trust and confidence in the product's capabilities.

4. **Establishing Credibility:** Jake subtly establishes credibility by mentioning a patented treatment process. While fictional, this implies a level of expertise and exclusivity. In practical sales, emphasizing product quality, certifications, or unique

production processes can enhance credibility. This reassures customers that they are making a sound and informed purchase.

5. **Word of Mouth Marketing:** Jake's customers become advocates, spreading the word, and attracting more buyers. Harnessing the power of satisfied customers as brand ambassadors is a potent real-world strategy. Encouraging reviews, testimonials, and referrals can create a positive feedback loop, contributing to sustained sales growth.

6. **Creating a Sense of Urgency:** The limited availability of Jake's sand, evidenced by the nearly empty stand by sunset, introduces an element of scarcity and urgency. This psychological trigger encourages customers to make decisions quickly. In practical sales, limited time offers, exclusive editions, or seasonal promotions can be used to create a sense of urgency and drive sales.

In conclusion, Jake Sanderson's success in selling sand on a beach is a testament to the effectiveness of strategic sales techniques. By identifying unique selling points, employing compelling storytelling, conducting live demonstrations, establishing credibility, leveraging word of mouth, and creating a sense of urgency, Jake displays a comprehensive approach to sales that can be adapted and applied to a wide range of practical products. This story serves as a playful yet insightful reminder that with creativity and strategic thinking, any product can find its niche and thrive in the market.

How Jake Identified the Unique Selling Point of his Products

In the quaint town of Shoreville, where the sun met the sea in a daily dance of hues, Jake Sanderson found himself pondering the impossible – selling sand on a beach. Determined to turn the mundane into a spectacle, Jake set out to identify the unique selling points (USPs) that would make his sand stand out in the vast grains of competition.

His journey began not with a pitch but with introspection. Jake spent days observing the beachgoers, studying their interactions with the sand, and listening to their desires. What did people want from the sand that they could not already find in abundance around them?

One sunny afternoon, as he watched children constructing sandcastles near the shoreline, a spark of inspiration ignited within Jake. He noticed the inevitable fate of their creations – washed away by the relentless tide. It was in that moment that he saw the potential for a USP: a sand that defied the laws of the ocean, a sandcastle sanctuary impervious to the tides.

With this revelation, Jake rushed back to his makeshift office, a small beachside hut, armed with newfound purpose. He scribbled down notes, envisioning the WetWonder – a sand that clung together, resisting the pull of the waves. This was to be the first unique selling point, a game-changer for beach enthusiasts.

But Jake was not satisfied with stopping there. He knew that a single USP might capture attention, but it would not hold it for long. So, he delved deeper into the potential desires of his customers. Why did people come to the beach, and what would make their experience even more enjoyable?

As he mulled over these questions, Jake envisioned a second variation of his sand. This one, he called the DryDream – a sand that offered unparalleled comfort for those seeking pure relaxation. A sand that would not stick to the skin, creating a personal beach oasis.

With the WetWonder and the DryDream identified, Jake had not one but two USPs that addressed the desires and pain points of his potential customers. The WetWonder catered to the creative spirits longing for sandcastle longevity, while the DryDream appealed to those seeking a blissful, sand-free escape.

Armed with his dual USPs, Jake began crafting his sales pitch. He knew he had something extraordinary, something that could turn heads and defy expectations. He practiced his pitch in front of the mirror, refining the words that would convey the magic of his sand to the sceptics and enthusiasts alike.

The day arrived when Jake set up his stand on the bustling beach, banners proudly proclaiming the WetWonder and the DryDream. As he spoke passionately about the sands that defied the ordinary, he saw the spark of interest in the eyes of the crowd.

Little did they know that behind Jake's charismatic pitch was the careful identification of unique selling points – the WetWonder and the DryDream – sands that would not only redefine their beach experience but also become the cornerstone of Jake Sanderson's improbable success in selling what was once considered impossible: sand on a beach.

How Jake created a Compelling Story for his Products

With his unique selling points identified, Jake Sanderson realized that to truly captivate his audience, he needed more than just features and benefits; he needed a compelling story that would elevate his sand from mere grains to a beachside sensation.

As the sun dipped low over the horizon, casting a warm glow on Shoreville's sandy shores, Jake sat down to weave the narrative that would breathe life into his product. He thought about the childhood joy of building sandcastles and the inevitable disappointment as the tide swept them away. That became the emotional core of his story – a tale of resilience and triumph over the forces of nature.

In his story, the WetWonder was not just sand; it was the hero in a seaside saga. Jake described the countless hours spent researching and developing a formula that would make sandcastles withstand the relentless onslaught of the waves. He spoke of late nights tinkering in his beachside hut, the scent of saltwater lingering in the air as he perfected the secret treatment process.

To illustrate the power of the WetWonder, Jake crafted an engaging demonstration. He sculpted intricate sandcastles, each one standing tall and proud as the waves crashed against them. The crowd watched in awe as the WetWonder held its ground, turning a simple beach activity into a triumphant battle of creativity against nature.

As for the DryDream, Jake took a different storytelling approach. He painted a picture of serene relaxation, describing the desire for a beach experience free from the inconveniences of sticky sand. He spoke of creating a haven for beachgoers, where the DryDream sand offered a soft, luxurious surface that enhanced the pleasure of soaking up the sun.

To make his story even more memorable, Jake incorporated the local charm of Shoreville. He shared anecdotes about the town's rich history of embracing the sea, drawing parallels between the resilience of the community and the steadfastness of his sands. This added a personal touch, making customers feel like they were not just buying sand but becoming a part of a coastal legacy.

The culmination of Jake's storytelling efforts was a narrative that transformed his sand from a commodity into an experience. He spoke with passion, infusing his words with the same enthusiasm that fuelled his journey from the concept of selling sand on a beach to the reality of creating an irresistible product.

When the first rays of dawn kissed the shore the next day, Jake stood by his stand, ready to share his story with the world. As he spoke of WetWonder's defiance against the tide and the DryDream's promise of unparalleled comfort, he watched as the audience became not just customers but participants in the narrative of his extraordinary sands.

In the end, it was not just about selling sand on a beach; it was about inviting people to be a part of something magical, a story where grains of sand transformed into the building blocks of unforgettable moments by the sea. Jake Sanderson had successfully turned his product into a tale, and in doing so, he had not only sold sand but woven a narrative that would linger in the memories of beachgoers for years to come.

How Jake developed his Demonstration Skills and Showmanship

With his compelling story carefully crafted, Jake Sanderson turned his attention to the pivotal moment of his sales pitch – the live demonstration. He understood that to truly captivate his audience, he needed to display the magic of the WetWonder in a way that would leave an indelible impression on beachgoers.

In the early morning hours, before the beach was buzzing with activity, Jake gathered his tools and materials. Buckets of WetWonder sand were artfully arranged, and he took a moment to appreciate the significance of what he was about to do. This demonstration was not just about building sandcastles; it was about proving that his product could defy the natural order of the beach.

To add an element of suspense and build anticipation, Jake decided to begin his pitch without immediately revealing the WetWonder's unique properties. He spoke passionately about the childhood joy of building sandcastles, the disappointment of watching them crumble, and the relentless determination that fuelled his quest for the perfect sand.

As the crowd leaned in, curious and eager, Jake theatrically unveiled the first pile of WetWonder sand. He let the grains cascade through his fingers, emphasizing the fine texture and quality. The audience, now fully engaged, could feel the anticipation in the air.

Before starting the demonstration, Jake engaged the crowd with a touch of humour. He cracked jokes about the perils of traditional sandcastles, drawing laughter from the onlookers. This not only lightened the atmosphere but also created a connection between Jake and his audience, making them more receptive to the upcoming spectacle.

Now, it was time for the main event. With a dramatic sweep of his arm, Jake began sculpting an intricate sandcastle. The crowd watched with bated breath as the structure took shape. With each careful pat and sculpted detail, Jake explained the science behind the WetWonder – the secret treatment process that transformed ordinary sand into a force to be reckoned with.

As he finished the sandcastle, Jake stepped back, inviting the audience to witness the spectacle. The waves crashed against the shore, but the WetWonder stood firm. Gasps of amazement and applause erupted from the crowd. Jake's showmanship had transformed a simple demonstration into a captivating performance.

Buoyed by the success of the WetWonder demonstration, Jake seamlessly transitioned to the DryDream segment of his pitch. He laid out the dry sand, inviting beachgoers to experience the unmatched comfort for themselves. With the same enthusiasm and flair, he displayed the softness of the DryDream, creating a haven for relaxation amid the sun-soaked sands.

In the end, Jake's preparation and showmanship had elevated his sales pitch from a mere product presentation to a memorable beachside spectacle. The combination of a compelling story, a dramatic unveiling, and an engaging demonstration had captured the hearts and imaginations of the crowd. Jake Sanderson had not only sold sand on a beach; he had orchestrated an experience that transcended the ordinary, leaving a lasting impression on everyone who witnessed the magic of WetWonder and the comfort of DryDream.

How Jake triumphed at Establishing Credibility

With the crowd still buzzing from the spectacle of WetWonder and the blissful comfort of DryDream, Jake Sanderson recognized the importance of establishing credibility to solidify the trust of his intrigued audience. He knew that to turn curious onlookers into confident buyers, he needed to convey the expertise and reliability behind his extraordinary sands.

As the sun climbed higher in the sky, Jake began the next phase of his pitch. He gestured to a small table beside him, where a display displayed the tools of his trade – scientific documents, diagrams, and certificates. This, he explained, was the culmination of years of research and development that went into perfecting the WetWonder and the DryDream.

To add a touch of authenticity, Jake described the challenges he faced during the developmental phase. He spoke of late nights spent experimenting in his beachside hut, the trial and error that led to the patented treatment process, and the collaboration with experts in the field of sand science (a term he playfully coined to emphasize the seriousness of his endeavour).

As Jake spoke, he carefully explained the intricacies of the treatment process, breaking down complex concepts into easily digestible information. He pointed out specific features on the scientific documents, highlighting the attention to detail that went into creating a sand that defied the ordinary.

To further establish credibility, Jake shared testimonials from early users of WetWonder and DryDream. He recounted stories of families building sandcastles that endured the entire day, of sunbathers revelling in the comfort of DryDream, and of the positive impact his sands had on the beach experience of countless individuals.

To address any lingering scepticism, Jake invited questions from the crowd. He responded with a mix of enthusiasm and expertise, reinforcing the credibility of his product with well-informed answers. The more technical inquiries were met with detailed explanations, displaying Jake's deep understanding of the science behind his sands.

As the presentation unfolded, the audience began to see Jake not just as a salesperson but as a passionate innovator dedicated to enhancing their beach experience. The combination of scientific credibility, personal anecdotes, and positive user testimonials created a compelling narrative that instilled trust in the minds of potential customers.

By the time Jake concluded the credibility segment of his pitch, the once-sceptical beachgoers had transformed into a receptive audience. They saw WetWonder and DryDream not as mere products but as the result of meticulous research, a commitment to quality, and a genuine passion for delivering an unparalleled beach experience.

With credibility firmly established, Jake Sanderson had successfully positioned his sands as not just a beach commodity but as a product backed by knowledge, expertise, and a proven track record. The journey from selling sand on a beach to selling a revolutionary beach experience was now one step closer to reality.

How Jake capitalised on Word-of-Mouth Marketing

With credibility firmly established and the crowd now entranced by the promise of WetWonder and DryDream, Jake Sanderson recognized the power of word-of-mouth marketing in propelling his sands to newfound heights. He understood that turning satisfied customers into vocal advocates would be the catalyst for the success of his improbable venture.

As the beachgoers lingered, some already clutching their newly acquired buckets of WetWonder and DryDream, Jake strategically employed a key element of his marketing plan – the encouragement of positive word of mouth. With a genuine smile, he addressed the audience.

"Friends, I know you've just experienced something extraordinary. WetWonder and DryDream are not just sands; they are a revolution in beach enjoyment. But don't take my word for it; let the sands speak for themselves."

Jake invited those who had made a purchase to share their thoughts with the rest of the crowd. A few eager customers stepped forward, sharing their immediate impressions and newfound delight with the WetWonder and DryDream. Their testimonials ranged from the joy of building sandcastles that stood defiant against the tide to the pure relaxation of lounging on the DryDream.

The authenticity of these testimonials resonated with the onlookers, turning casual interest into genuine curiosity. Jake, ever the showman, amplified the impact by offering a small incentive for those who shared their experiences. A spontaneous wave of enthusiasm swept through the crowd as more people stepped forward to express their delight.

To further leverage the power of word of mouth, Jake introduced a referral program. He encouraged customers to bring friends and family to his stand, promising additional perks for both the referrer and the new customer. This not only incentivized existing customers to spread the word but also expanded Jake's reach within the beach community.

To keep the momentum going, Jake set up a simple yet effective feedback mechanism. He distributed small cards that allowed customers to jot down their thoughts and suggestions. The promise of potential improvements and future enhancements fuelled a sense of ownership among the buyers, turning them into collaborators in the ongoing development of WetWonder and DryDream.

As the day progressed, the beach became a lively canvas of conversation, with beachgoers enthusiastically sharing their experiences with Jake's extraordinary sands. Laughter and positive chatter surrounded the stand, creating an atmosphere that was not just about selling a product but fostering a community united by a shared appreciation for beach innovation.

By sunset, Jake Sanderson watched with satisfaction as the beachgoers, now advocates for WetWonder and DryDream, dispersed across the shoreline. The seeds of word-of-mouth marketing had been sown, and the once-impossible task of selling sand on a beach had transformed into a beachside sensation, fuelled by the genuine excitement and endorsement of those who had experienced the magic firsthand.

Jake knew that the success of WetWonder and DryDream would continue to ripple through the beach community, spreading like the gentle waves that lapped at the shore. Word of mouth, the most authentic and powerful form of marketing, had become the catalyst for his sands' journey from an idea to an indispensable part of the beach experience.

How Jake Created a Sense of Urgency

As the sun dipped lower on the horizon, casting a warm golden glow over Shoreville's beach, Jake Sanderson realized that to solidify the success of WetWonder and DryDream, he needed to infuse a sense of urgency into his sales strategy. The allure of his extraordinary sands needed to be coupled with the immediacy of the opportunity.

With a twinkle in his eye and an air of anticipation, Jake gathered the remaining beachgoers around his stand. He knew that creating a sense of urgency would not only drive sales but also enhance the overall experience of acquiring WetWonder and DryDream.

"Dear friends," Jake began, his voice carrying a sense of excitement, "what you've witnessed today is just the beginning of something truly remarkable. WetWonder and DryDream have captured your imagination, but I must let you in on a little secret – the magic doesn't last forever."

He went on to explain that due to the overwhelming demand and the limited availability of the specially treated sand, there were only a finite number of buckets left. The crowd, now fully engaged, listened intently as Jake painted a picture of exclusivity and the fleeting opportunity to be among the privileged few to own these extraordinary sands.

To intensify the sense of urgency, Jake introduced a limited time offer. Those who purchased WetWonder and DryDream within the next hour would receive a special bonus – an exclusive accessory for building the most magnificent sandcastles. This time-sensitive incentive, coupled with the fear of missing out on the revolutionary sands, spurred a flurry of activity around Jake's stand.

As beachgoers rushed to secure their buckets, Jake's charisma and urgency-driven pitch reached its peak. He reminded the crowd that they were not just buying sand; they were investing in an experience, a chance to elevate their beach days to unprecedented levels of enjoyment.

To further heighten the urgency, Jake announced that once the current stock of WetWonder and DryDream was depleted, it would be some time before the next batch would be available. This scarcity factor not only accelerated the pace of sales but also added an element of prestige to those who had acted swiftly.

As the final buckets of WetWonder and DryDream were claimed, Jake took a moment to express his gratitude to the enthusiastic crowd. He assured them that their decision to seize the moment and be part of this beachside revolution would be rewarded with countless hours of joy and relaxation.

As the sun dipped below the horizon, casting vibrant hues across the sky, the beachgoers dispersed, each carrying a bucket of WetWonder or DryDream, a tangible token of their decision to embrace the extraordinary. Jake Sanderson, with a stand nearly empty but pockets of Shoreville now filled with his revolutionary sands, knew that the combination of urgency, exclusivity, and excitement had turned an improbable venture into a resounding success.

The story of selling sand on a beach had evolved into a narrative of seizing the moment, of creating an experience that was not just about the sands but about embracing the magic of the present. And as the echoes of satisfied customers and the allure of WetWonder and DryDream lingered on the shore, Jake stood by his stand, savouring the satisfaction of having transformed the impossible into a moment of beachside brilliance.

Identifying Unique Selling Points (USPs)

Identifying Unique Selling Points (USPs) is a critical skill for any salesperson aiming to distinguish their product or service in a crowded market. A USP is what sets a product apart from its competitors, creating a compelling reason for customers to choose one offering over another. Here is a detailed summary on how a salesperson can effectively identify and leverage USPs:

1. **Market Research:** Begin by conducting thorough market research to understand the landscape of your industry. Analyse competitors to identify what they are offering, their strengths, and areas where they may be lacking. Recognizing gaps in the market allows you to tailor your USPs to meet unmet needs.

2. **Customer Needs Analysis:** Understand your target audience's pain points and desires. Conduct surveys, interviews, and gather feedback to identify what customers value the most in a product or service. Knowing the specific needs of your audience helps in tailoring USPs that directly address and fulfil those needs.

3. **Product Features and Benefits:** Evaluate the features and benefits of your product or service. What makes it unique or superior? This could be a distinctive feature, a proprietary technology, exceptional quality, or a specific benefit that directly addresses customer concerns. Highlight these aspects as potential USPs.

4. **Quality and Performance:** Assess the quality and performance of your offering. If it surpasses industry standards or provides a superior experience, these attributes can serve as strong USPs. Emphasize how your product outperforms others in the market.

5. **Price Positioning:** Consider your pricing strategy in relation to the competition. If your product offers better value for money, whether through lower prices or additional features at the same price, this can be a powerful USP. Alternatively, if

your product is positioned as a premium offering, emphasize the exclusivity and added value it brings.

6. **Innovation and Uniqueness:** Highlight any innovations or unique elements that set your product apart. Whether it is a groundbreaking technology, a novel design, or an exclusive feature, emphasizing the uniqueness of your offering can attract customers looking for something different.

7. **Customer Testimonials and Success Stories:** Leverage positive customer testimonials and success stories. Real-world examples of how your product or service has benefited others provide tangible evidence of its value and can serve as persuasive USPs.

8. **Brand Reputation:** If your brand has a strong reputation for reliability, trustworthiness, or exceptional customer service, use these aspects as USPs. A positive brand image can influence purchasing decisions and set your product apart from competitors.

9. **Sustainability and Social Responsibility:** In an era where environmental and social consciousness are on the rise, a commitment to sustainability or social responsibility can be a compelling USP. Highlight eco-friendly practices, ethical sourcing, or community involvement to appeal to conscious consumers.

10. **Adaptability and Flexibility:** If your product offers versatility or can be tailored to individual needs, emphasize its adaptability as a USP. Products or services that can meet diverse customer requirements often stand out in the market.

In summary, identifying USPs involves a strategic combination of understanding market dynamics, customer needs, and the unique qualities of your product or service. By effectively communicating these differentiators, a salesperson can create a compelling value proposition that resonates with customers and sets their offering apart in a competitive landscape.

Market Research

Market research is a foundational and indispensable aspect of a salesperson's toolkit, providing valuable insights into the dynamics of the industry, customer behaviour, and competitive landscape. A thorough summary of market research for a salesperson includes:

1. **Understanding the Market Landscape:** Begin by gaining a comprehensive understanding of the market in which your product or service operates. This involves studying the overall industry size, trends, and growth projections. Recognize key players, market segments, and any emerging opportunities or threats.

2. **Competitor Analysis:** Conduct a detailed analysis of competitors to identify their strengths, weaknesses, strategies, and market positioning. This involves studying their product offerings, pricing strategies, distribution channels, and marketing tactics. Understanding the competitive landscape helps you position your product more effectively.

3. **Customer Profiling:** Create detailed customer profiles to understand the demographics, preferences, and behaviour of your target audience. This involves researching factors such as age, gender, income levels, geographic location, and purchasing habits. The more precise your customer profiles, the better you can tailor your sales approach.

4. **Identifying Customer Needs and Pain Points:** Through surveys, interviews, and data analysis, identify the specific needs, challenges, and pain points of your target customers. This information helps you tailor your product or service to address real customer concerns, making your sales pitch more relevant.

5. **Product Positioning:** Analyse how similar products or services are positioned in the market. Assess the unique selling propositions (USPs) of competitors and determine

how your offering can differentiate itself. Understanding the existing positioning landscape is crucial for effective marketing and sales strategies.

6. **Pricing Strategies:** Examine the pricing strategies of competitors to determine the prevailing price points in the market. Assess whether your product should be positioned as a premium offering, a budget-friendly alternative, or somewhere in between. Pricing research helps optimize your product's value proposition.

7. **Distribution Channels:** Study the distribution channels used by competitors and evaluate their effectiveness. Understanding how products reach customers allows you to optimize your own distribution strategy. This may involve considering partnerships, online platforms, retail outlets, or direct sales.

8. **SWOT Analysis:** Conduct a SWOT analysis (Strengths, Weaknesses, Opportunities, Threats) for your product or service. This internal and external assessment helps you identify areas where you can capitalize on strengths, mitigate weaknesses, seize opportunities, and guard against threats.

9. **Trend Analysis:** Stay abreast of industry trends, technological advancements, and changes in consumer behaviour. Being aware of evolving trends allows you to adapt your sales strategies and product offerings to align with current market demands.

10. **Regulatory Environment:** Understand the regulatory environment in which your product operates. Complying with regulations is essential for long-term success. Additionally, being aware of upcoming changes or legislative trends can help you anticipate and navigate potential challenges.

11. **Feedback from Existing Customers:** Gather feedback from existing customers to assess their satisfaction levels, identify

areas for improvement, and understand their evolving needs. Satisfied customers can become brand advocates, while constructive feedback informs product enhancements.

In summary, market research for a salesperson involves a comprehensive exploration of the market landscape, competition, and customer dynamics. By leveraging the insights gained through market research, sales professionals can develop targeted strategies, refine their value propositions, and stay agile in a dynamic business environment.

Customer Needs Analysis

Customer Needs Analysis is a pivotal aspect of a salesperson's role, aiming to understand the specific requirements, preferences, and challenges of potential customers. A detailed summary of Customer Needs Analysis for a salesperson encompasses the following key elements:

1. **Active Listening:** The foundation of Customer Needs Analysis lies in active listening. Salespeople must attentively listen to customers during conversations, whether in-person, over the phone, or through digital channels. This involves paying attention to verbal cues, tone, and non-verbal communication to gather comprehensive insights.

2. **Open-Ended Questions:** Employing open-ended questions is essential for encouraging customers to express their thoughts and needs freely. These questions prompt more detailed responses and provide a deeper understanding of the customer's requirements. Open-ended questions often begin with words like "how," "what," or "why."

3. **Probing for Pain Points:** Delve into the customer's pain points and challenges. Understanding the problems, they face allows you to position your product or service as a solution.

This requires a sensitive and empathetic approach to uncovering issues that may not be immediately apparent.

4. **Building Rapport:** Establishing a strong rapport with customers is crucial for creating an environment where they feel comfortable sharing their needs. A positive and trustworthy relationship facilitates open communication and enhances the accuracy of the information gathered during the analysis.

5. **Understanding Decision-Making Criteria:** Identify the criteria that influence the customer's decision-making process. This includes factors such as price, quality, brand reputation, customer support, and specific features. Understanding these criteria helps tailor the sales pitch to align with the customer's priorities.

6. **Clarifying and Summarizing:** Throughout the conversation, periodically clarify and summarize the information shared by the customer. This not only demonstrates active engagement but also ensures mutual understanding. Clear communication helps avoid misunderstandings and ensures that the salesperson accurately grasps the customer's needs.

7. **Adapting Communication Style:** Tailor your communication style to match the preferences of the customer. Some customers may prefer detailed explanations, while others may appreciate a more concise and to-the-point approach. Adapting your style ensures that you effectively convey information in a manner that resonates with the customer.

8. **Utilizing Technology and Data:** Leverage technology and data analytics tools to gather insights into customer behaviour, preferences, and historical interactions. Analysing data can provide a more holistic view of customer needs and enable salespeople to personalize their approach based on past interactions.

9. **Collaborative Problem-Solving:** Position the sales process as a collaborative effort to solve the customer's challenges. By framing the interaction as a partnership, the salesperson fosters a sense of shared responsibility, reinforcing the idea that the product or service is tailored to meet the customer's unique needs.

10. **Prioritizing Needs:** Not all customer needs are of equal importance. Salespeople must identify and prioritize the most critical needs that align with the customer's goals and expectations. This prioritization guides the sales strategy, ensuring that the focus is on addressing the most impactful requirements.

11. **Feedback Loop:** Establish a feedback loop with customers to validate the accuracy of the needs analysis. Regular check-ins and follow-up conversations provide opportunities to refine the understanding of customer needs as their priorities may evolve over time.

In summary, Customer Needs Analysis is an ongoing, dynamic process that requires active listening, empathy, and adaptability. By gaining a deep understanding of customer needs, salespeople can tailor their approach, effectively position their offerings, and ultimately build long-lasting, mutually beneficial relationships with customers.

Product Features and Benefits

Effectively understanding and communicating product features and benefits is a cornerstone of successful salesmanship. Here is a detailed summary of how a salesperson can navigate and leverage product features and benefits:

1. **Thorough Product Knowledge:** A salesperson must have a comprehensive understanding of the product, including its features, specifications, and functionalities. This knowledge serves as the foundation for effective communication with customers.

2. **Distinguishing Features from Benefits:** Features are the specific characteristics of a product, while benefits are the advantages or positive outcomes that customers gain from those features. A salesperson should be adept at distinguishing and articulating both features and benefits to create a compelling value proposition.

3. **Customer-Centric Approach:** Frame the presentation of features and benefits from the customer's perspective. Highlight how each feature addresses a specific need or solves a problem for the customer. This customer-centric approach makes the product more relevant and appealing.

4. **Prioritizing Key Features:** Identify the key features that set the product apart from competitors or directly address customer pain points. Prioritize these features in your communication to create a strong initial impression and capture the customer's attention.

5. **Aligning Features with Customer Needs:** Tailor the presentation of features to align with the specific needs and preferences of each customer. By customizing the discussion to address individual requirements, the salesperson can demonstrate how the product is uniquely suited to meet the customer's goals.

6. **Emphasizing Unique Selling Points (USPs):** Highlight the product's unique selling points (USPs) derived from its features. Whether it is a technological innovation, a proprietary process, or an exclusive feature, USPs differentiate the product in the market and should be a focal point in the sales pitch.

7. **Translating Features into Benefits:** Articulate how each product feature translates into a tangible benefit for the customer. For example, if a laptop has a fast processor (feature), explain that this results in quicker task execution and enhanced productivity (benefit).

8. **Storytelling:** Incorporate storytelling to illustrate how the product features have positively impacted other customers. Real-life examples and case studies provide context and make the benefits more relatable, fostering a deeper connection with the customer.

9. **Handling Objections Proactively:** Anticipate potential objections and address them proactively by highlighting features that directly counter or mitigate concerns. This proactive approach builds confidence in the product and the salesperson's expertise.

10. **Visual Aids and Demonstrations:** Utilize visual aids, product demonstrations, and interactive tools to enhance the understanding of product features. Visual representation makes complex features more accessible and reinforces the benefits through a practical demonstration.

11. **Educational Approach:** Take on an educational role by explaining how each feature works and the value it adds. This approach positions the salesperson as a trusted advisor, fostering a sense of trust and credibility.

12. **Adaptability to Customer Knowledge Levels:** Tailor the level of technical detail to match the customer's knowledge and familiarity with the product category. Some customers may appreciate in-depth technical information, while others prefer a more straightforward explanation.

13. **Closing with Benefits:** When closing a sale, re-emphasize the key benefits that resonate most with the customer. This reinforces the value proposition and helps in sealing the deal.

In summary, effective communication of product features and benefits requires a nuanced understanding of the product, the ability to align features with customer needs, and skilful articulation of how these features translate into tangible advantages. A salesperson's proficiency in conveying the value proposition can significantly impact the customer's perception and decision-making process.

Quality and Performance

Quality and performance are critical aspects that a salesperson must emphasize to instil confidence in customers and differentiate their product or service. Here is a detailed summary of how a salesperson can navigate and leverage quality and performance in sales:

1. **Thorough Understanding of Product Quality:** A salesperson must have an in-depth understanding of the product's quality standards. This includes knowledge of manufacturing processes, materials used, and any certifications or quality assurance measures in place.

2. **Articulating Quality Standards:** Clearly communicate the quality standards that the product adheres to. This may include industry certifications, compliance with regulations, or internal quality control measures. Emphasize how these standards contribute to the overall reliability of the product.

3. **Performance Specifications:** Detail the specific performance specifications of the product. This could involve technical aspects such as speed, durability, efficiency, or any other parameters relevant to the product category. Providing concrete performance metrics helps customers assess the product's capabilities.

4. **Comparative Analysis:** Conduct a comparative analysis with competitors to highlight the superior quality and performance of your product. This can involve displaying specific features, performance metrics, or customer testimonials that demonstrate a competitive advantage.

5. **User Testimonials and Reviews:** Leverage positive user testimonials and reviews that emphasize the product's quality and performance. Real-life experiences from satisfied customers serve as powerful endorsements and build trust in the reliability of the product.

6. **Warranty and Guarantee Policies:** Clearly explain the warranty and guarantee policies associated with the product. A robust warranty or guarantee can be a reassuring factor for customers, demonstrating the seller's confidence in the product's durability and performance.

7. **Product Demonstrations:** Conduct product demonstrations that display its quality and performance in real-time. Whether it is a physical product or a software solution, allowing customers to see the product in action provides tangible evidence of its capabilities.

8. **Case Studies:** Develop case studies that highlight instances where the product's quality and performance led to significant positive outcomes for customers. Case studies add a storytelling element, making the benefits of the product more tangible and relatable.

9. **Continuous Improvement:** Communicate the company's commitment to continuous improvement in product quality and performance. Assure customers that the organization actively seeks feedback, invests in research and development, and consistently works towards enhancing the product.

10. **Industry Recognitions and Awards:** If applicable, highlight any industry recognitions or awards that the product has received for its quality and performance. External validations add credibility and serve as independent endorsements of the product's excellence.

11. **Transparency in Communication:** Be transparent about the product's limitations and set realistic expectations. This honesty builds trust with customers and prevents potential dissatisfaction if expectations are not met.

12. **Training and Support Services:** Emphasize the training and support services available to customers. This not only reinforces the commitment to ensuring optimal product

performance but also provides customers with resources to maximize their investment.

13. **Post-Purchase Follow-Up:** Conduct post-purchase follow-ups to gather feedback on the product's performance. This not only shows dedication to customer satisfaction but also provides insights for future improvements.

In summary, a salesperson's ability to effectively communicate the quality and performance of a product is crucial for building customer confidence and facilitating purchasing decisions. By displaying the tangible benefits and demonstrating the product's capabilities, a salesperson can position the offering as a reliable and high-performing solution in the market.

Price Positioning

Price positioning is a strategic element of sales that involves determining the optimal pricing strategy for a product or service. Here is a detailed summary of how a salesperson can navigate and leverage price positioning:

1. **Understanding Market Dynamics:** A salesperson needs to have a comprehensive understanding of the market, including the pricing strategies of competitors, consumer purchasing behaviour, and overall economic conditions. This knowledge forms the basis for effective price positioning.

2. **Cost Analysis:** Conduct a thorough cost analysis to determine the production, distribution, and marketing expenses associated with the product or service. This analysis helps set a baseline for pricing and ensures that the pricing strategy is financially sustainable.

3. **Value-Based Pricing:** Consider adopting a value-based pricing strategy, where the price is determined by the perceived value of the product or service to the customer. Highlight the unique features, benefits, and advantages that justify a higher price point compared to competitors.

4. **Competitive Benchmarking:** Analyse the pricing strategies of competitors to determine where the product or service stands in relation to similar offerings in the market. This involves assessing whether the product will be positioned as a premium, mid-range, or budget option.

5. **Differentiation:** Emphasize the unique selling points (USPs) that differentiate the product or service from competitors. If the product offers exclusive features, superior quality, or additional benefits, these differentiators can justify a higher price.

6. **Psychological Pricing:** Leverage psychological pricing strategies to influence consumer perceptions. This can include pricing just below a round number (e.g., $99.99 instead of $100) or using tiered pricing structures to create the perception of value.

7. **Bundling and Upselling:** Consider bundling products or services to create perceived value and offer customers a more attractive deal. Additionally, explore opportunities for upselling by presenting higher-tier options with added features or benefits.

8. **Discounts and Promotions:** Strategically use discounts and promotions to drive sales and attract price-sensitive customers. However, ensure that discounts do not compromise the perceived value of the product or erode profit margins.

9. **Tiered Pricing Models:** Implement tiered pricing models that cater to different customer segments. This allows customers to choose a pricing tier that aligns with their budget while providing opportunities for the salesperson to maximize revenue.

10. **Anchor Pricing:** Use anchor pricing by prominently displaying a higher-priced option alongside the main product.

This can influence customers to perceive the main product as a more reasonable and attractive choice.

11. **Dynamic Pricing:** Explore dynamic pricing strategies that allow for flexibility in adjusting prices based on demand, seasonality, or other market conditions. This adaptive approach enables the product to remain competitive and responsive to changing dynamics.

12. **Transparent Communication:** Communicate transparently about the pricing strategy with customers. Clearly articulate the value they will receive at the specified price point and address any potential concerns regarding the cost.

13. **Customer Segmentation:** Segment customers based on their willingness and ability to pay. This allows for targeted pricing strategies that align with the diverse needs and preferences of different customer segments.

14. **Long-Term Profitability:** While short-term sales are important, prioritize long-term profitability. Ensure that the pricing strategy supports sustained business growth and covers all associated costs to maintain a healthy profit margin.

In summary, price positioning involves a strategic balance between understanding market dynamics, displaying value, and aligning the pricing strategy with customer expectations. A salesperson's ability to effectively position the product or service in the market through pricing can influence consumer perceptions, drive sales, and contribute to overall business success.

Innovation and Uniqueness

Innovation and uniqueness play a pivotal role in the success of sales efforts. A salesperson's ability to effectively convey the innovative and unique aspects of a product or service can significantly influence customer perception and purchasing decisions. Here is a detailed summary of how a salesperson can navigate and leverage innovation and uniqueness:

1. **Product Familiarity:** A salesperson must possess a deep understanding of the product's innovative features and unique selling points. Comprehensive product knowledge allows for confident and accurate communication with potential customers.

2. **Identifying Innovation:** Clearly identify and articulate the innovative elements of the product. This could involve technological advancements, unique design features, proprietary processes, or any distinctive aspects that set the product apart from competitors.

3. **Aligning Innovation with Customer Needs:** Tailor the discussion of innovation to align with the specific needs and pain points of the customer. Emphasize how the innovative features directly address challenges or enhance aspects of the customer's experience.

4. **Demonstrating Value:** Clearly communicate the value that the innovative features bring to the customer. Whether it is increased efficiency, cost savings, enhanced performance, or a unique experience, customers need to understand how innovation translates into tangible benefits.

5. **Visual Aids and Demonstrations:** Use visual aids, demonstrations, and interactive tools to display the innovative aspects of the product. Visual representation makes complex innovations more accessible and reinforces the benefits through practical demonstration.

6. **Comparative Advantage:** Conduct a comparative analysis with competitors to highlight the specific advantages that the product's innovation offers. This could involve displaying superior technology, more efficient processes, or any unique features that differentiate the product.

7. **Storytelling:** Incorporate storytelling to illustrate how the product's innovation has positively impacted other customers. Real-life examples and case studies provide context and make the benefits of the innovation more relatable.

8. **Continuous Improvement Narrative:** Communicate the company's commitment to continuous improvement and innovation. Assure customers that the organization actively seeks feedback, invests in research and development, and consistently works towards enhancing the product.

9. **Leveraging Testimonials and Reviews:** Leverage positive testimonials and reviews that specifically highlight the innovative features of the product. Customer endorsements serve as powerful social proof and build credibility around the product's uniqueness.

10. **Customization and Adaptability:** Emphasize any customization options or adaptability that the product offers. The ability to tailor the product to meet specific customer needs enhances its uniqueness and positions it as a flexible solution.

11. **Educational Approach:** Take on an educational role by explaining how the innovation works and the value it adds. This approach positions the salesperson as a trusted advisor, fostering a sense of trust and credibility.

12. **Addressing Potential Concerns:** Proactively address any potential concerns or misconceptions customers may have about the innovative features. Anticipating questions and providing clear, concise answers builds confidence in the product.

13. **Sustainability and Social Responsibility:** If applicable, highlight any innovative practices related to sustainability or social responsibility. Increasingly, customers are attracted to products that align with their values and demonstrate a commitment to making a positive impact.

14. **Future Roadmap:** Discuss the company's future plans for innovation. Assure customers that investing in the product means being part of an ongoing journey of improvement and staying at the forefront of industry advancements.

In summary, a salesperson's ability to effectively communicate the innovation and uniqueness of a product involves a combination of in-depth product knowledge, customer-centric communication, and the strategic use of visual aids and testimonials. By displaying how innovation directly benefits the customer and differentiates the product in the market, a salesperson can create a compelling narrative that resonates with potential buyers.

Customer Testimonials and Success Stories

Leveraging customer testimonials and success stories is a powerful strategy for salespeople to build trust, establish credibility, and demonstrate the value of a product or service. Here is a detailed summary of how a salesperson can effectively navigate and utilize customer testimonials and success stories:

1. **Collecting Diverse Testimonials:** Actively seek testimonials from a diverse range of customers. Ensure that the testimonials represent various industries, use cases, and customer profiles. This diversity enhances the credibility of the endorsements and makes them relatable to a broader audience.

2. **Authenticity and Transparency:** Prioritize authenticity in testimonials. Genuine, heartfelt endorsements from

customers resonate more effectively with potential buyers. Avoid overly scripted or exaggerated testimonials, as authenticity contributes to trust-building.

3. **Highlighting Specific Benefits:** Encourage customers to focus on specific benefits they have experienced with the product or service. Whether it is increased efficiency, cost savings, improved outcomes, or any other tangible result, testimonials should articulate the positive impact on the customer's business or life.

4. **Before-and-After Narratives:** Craft testimonials in a narrative format, detailing the customer's situation before using the product or service and the positive transformation afterward. This storytelling approach engages potential customers and illustrates the journey of improvement.

5. **Use of Quotes and Statistics:** Extract impactful quotes and statistics from testimonials that succinctly capture the essence of the customer's experience. These bite-sized pieces of information can be prominently featured in marketing materials, presentations, and sales pitches.

6. **Incorporating Success Stories:** Develop comprehensive success stories that provide in-depth insights into how the product or service solved a customer's challenges. Success stories typically include background information, the customer's specific needs, the implemented solution, and the resulting benefits.

7. **Video Testimonials:** Explore the use of video testimonials for a more engaging and dynamic presentation. Video allows customers to convey their emotions and enthusiasm, creating a more personal connection with potential buyers. Well-produced video testimonials can be powerful assets in marketing efforts.

8. **Permission and Compliance:** Ensure that you have permission from customers to use their testimonials and

success stories in marketing materials. Comply with any legal or privacy considerations and respect the confidentiality of sensitive information.

9. **Strategic Placement in Marketing Collateral:** Integrate customer testimonials strategically into various marketing collateral, including websites, brochures, presentations, and social media. Well-placed endorsements serve as persuasive tools throughout the buyer's journey.

10. **Tailoring Testimonials to Target Audience:** Customize testimonials to resonate with specific target audiences. If possible, display testimonials from customers who share similar demographics, industries, or challenges with potential buyers. This tailored approach enhances relatability.

11. **Response to Common Objections:** Address common objections or concerns that potential customers might have through testimonials. If a testimonial addresses and overcomes a specific objection, it provides reassurance to potential buyers.

12. **Encouraging Two-Way Communication:** Foster a two-way communication channel with customers who provide testimonials. This not only allows for ongoing feedback but also creates a positive relationship, making customers more willing to participate in future endorsements.

13. **Integration with Sales Pitches:** Seamlessly integrate customer testimonials into sales pitches. Whether in-person or virtual, incorporating real-world examples of success can significantly enhance the persuasiveness of the sales presentation.

14. **Continuous Gathering of Testimonials:** Make testimonial collection an ongoing process. Regularly seek feedback from customers and encourage them to share their success stories. This ensures a steady stream of fresh and relevant endorsements to bolster sales efforts.

In summary, customer testimonials and success stories are invaluable tools for salespeople. By prioritizing authenticity, diversity, and strategic use of these endorsements, sales professionals can build a compelling narrative that instils confidence in potential buyers and drives successful sales outcomes.

Brand Reputation

Brand reputation is a critical element in sales, influencing customer trust, loyalty, and purchase decisions. Here is a detailed summary of how a salesperson can navigate and leverage brand reputation effectively:

1. **Understanding the Brand:** A salesperson should have a deep understanding of the brand they represent, including its history, values, mission, and overall positioning in the market. This knowledge forms the foundation for effective communication with customers.

2. **Consistency in Brand Messaging:** Ensure consistency in brand messaging across all communication channels. A cohesive and unified brand message reinforces customer perception and builds a strong, recognizable brand identity.

3. **Highlighting Positive Attributes:** Emphasize the positive attributes and unique selling points that contribute to the brand's positive reputation. This could include factors such as reliability, quality, innovation, customer service, or any other strengths that set the brand apart.

4. **Addressing Brand Weaknesses:** Acknowledge and address any potential weaknesses or challenges in the brand's reputation. Transparency about past issues, coupled with a commitment to improvement, can build trust with customers and mitigate concerns.

5. **Leveraging Brand Recognition:** Leverage the recognition and positive associations that come with an established

brand. If the brand is well-known or has a positive reputation in the market, salespeople should capitalize on this recognition to create trust and credibility.

6. **Customer Testimonials and Case Studies:** Incorporate customer testimonials and case studies that specifically highlight positive experiences with the brand. Real-world examples serve as powerful endorsements and contribute to the overall positive perception of the brand.

7. **Aligning with Brand Values:** Ensure that sales strategies and practices align with the brand's core values. Consistency between the salesperson's approach and the brand's values reinforces authenticity and strengthens the overall brand reputation.

8. **Social Proof and Online Presence:** Leverage social proof, such as positive reviews, ratings, and testimonials, to bolster the brand's online reputation. Actively manage online presence on review platforms and social media to respond to customer feedback and display the brand's commitment to customer satisfaction.

9. **Handling Negative Feedback:** Effectively manage and address negative feedback or criticisms. A prompt and constructive response to negative reviews or comments demonstrates a commitment to customer satisfaction and can turn a negative situation into a positive one.

10. **Training Sales Team on Brand Values:** Ensure that the sales team is well-trained on the brand's values, messaging, and customer service standards. A unified and knowledgeable sales team contributes to a positive customer experience and reinforces the brand's reputation.

11. **Educational Content:** Develop and share educational content that displays the brand's expertise in the industry. By positioning the brand as a thought leader, salespeople contribute to the overall positive perception of the brand.

12. **Networking and Relationship Building:** Actively engage in networking and relationship-building activities. Personal connections and positive interactions with clients contribute to the brand's reputation through word-of-mouth referrals and recommendations.

13. **Monitoring Industry Trends:** Stay informed about industry trends and developments. Being knowledgeable about the market landscape allows salespeople to position the brand as forward-thinking and adaptable, contributing to a positive reputation.

14. **Internal Communication:** Foster open communication within the organization to ensure that everyone is aligned with the brand's values and goals. A cohesive internal culture translates into a positive external reputation.

15. **Long-Term Focus:** Prioritize long-term brand building over short-term gains. Consistently delivering on promises, providing excellent customer service, and maintaining ethical business practices contribute to a sustained positive brand reputation.

In summary, a salesperson's role in leveraging brand reputation involves a combination of understanding, promoting, and aligning with the brand's values and strengths. By consistently reinforcing positive attributes, addressing challenges transparently, and actively contributing to a positive customer experience, sales professionals can enhance the overall reputation of the brand and drive successful sales outcomes.

Sustainability and Social Responsibility

Sustainability and social responsibility have become increasingly important considerations for consumers, influencing their purchasing decisions. Here is a detailed summary of how a salesperson can navigate and leverage sustainability and social responsibility effectively:

1. **Understanding Corporate Practices:** A salesperson should have a deep understanding of the company's sustainability initiatives and social responsibility practices. This knowledge forms the basis for aligning the product or service with the broader goals of responsible business practices.

2. **Communicating Environmental Impact:** Clearly communicate the environmental impact of the product or service. This could include details about eco-friendly materials, energy efficiency, reduced carbon footprint, or any other environmentally conscious features. Transparency in environmental claims is essential for building trust.

3. **Highlighting Social Impact:** Emphasize the positive social impact associated with the product or service. This may involve supporting fair labour practices, community development, or charitable initiatives. Articulating how the purchase contributes to social betterment can resonate with socially conscious consumers.

4. **Certifications and Standards:** Display any relevant certifications or adherence to industry standards related to sustainability and social responsibility. Certifications from recognized organizations add credibility and validate the company's commitment to responsible business practices.

5. **Educating Customers:** Take on an educational role by providing information about the broader implications of sustainable and socially responsible choices. This can include educating customers on the importance of sustainable sourcing, ethical production, and the positive impact of their purchasing decisions.

6. **Storytelling with Impact:** Incorporate storytelling to illustrate the company's journey toward sustainability and social responsibility. Real-life examples and case studies can

convey the impact of responsible business practices in a compelling and relatable way.

7. **Transparency in Supply Chain:** Communicate transparency in the supply chain, detailing efforts to ensure ethical sourcing and fair labour practices. A transparent supply chain reinforces the company's commitment to social responsibility and sustainability.

8. **Product Life Cycle Considerations:** Consider and communicate the entire life cycle of the product, from production to disposal. Highlighting efforts to minimize environmental impact at every stage contributes to a holistic narrative of sustainability.

9. **Customer Engagement in Sustainability:** Involve customers in the sustainability journey. Encourage them to participate in recycling programs, provide feedback on sustainable initiatives, or share their own experiences with socially responsible practices. This engagement fosters a sense of shared responsibility.

10. **Green Packaging and Practices:** Emphasize sustainable packaging materials and practices. This includes reducing packaging waste, utilizing recyclable materials, and exploring innovative packaging solutions that minimize environmental impact.

11. **Collaboration with Eco-Friendly Partners:** Highlight collaborations with suppliers and partners who share a commitment to sustainability. Demonstrating that the entire business ecosystem is aligned with responsible practices reinforces the brand's dedication to making a positive impact.

12. **Aligning with Customer Values:** Understand the values of the target customer base and tailor the messaging to align with those values. If sustainability and social responsibility are important to the customer, positioning the product as a reflection of those values can enhance its appeal.

13. **Measurable Impact Metrics:** Where possible, provide measurable metrics that display the impact of sustainable and socially responsible practices. This could include metrics related to carbon reduction, community development, or other key performance indicators that demonstrate tangible results.

14. **Continuous Improvement:** Communicate the company's commitment to continuous improvement in sustainability and social responsibility. This involves regularly assessing and enhancing practices to stay aligned with evolving industry standards and societal expectations.

15. **Adaptability to Market Trends:** Stay informed about emerging trends and preferences related to sustainability. Being adaptable and responsive to evolving market expectations ensures that the company remains a leader in responsible business practices.

In summary, a salesperson's role in leveraging sustainability and social responsibility involves effectively communicating the company's initiatives, aligning products with customer values, and contributing to a narrative of positive impact. By integrating these considerations into sales strategies, sales professionals can appeal to the growing segment of socially conscious consumers and drive meaningful, responsible purchasing decisions.

Adaptability and Flexibility

Adaptability and flexibility are crucial qualities for a salesperson, enabling them to navigate the dynamic and ever-changing landscape of sales. Here is a detailed summary of how a salesperson can effectively leverage adaptability and flexibility:

1. **Understanding Market Dynamics:** A salesperson must have a deep understanding of market trends, customer behaviours, and industry developments. Regularly staying informed about changes in the market allows for proactive adjustments to sales strategies.

2. **Agile Approach to Sales Strategies:** Adopt an agile approach to sales strategies. This involves the ability to quickly pivot and adjust tactics based on shifts in customer needs, competitive landscapes, or external factors that may impact the sales environment.

3. **Customizing Communication Styles:** Tailor communication styles to resonate with diverse customer personalities and preferences. Flexibility in communication, whether in-person, over the phone, or through digital channels, ensures that the salesperson can effectively connect with a wide range of clients.

4. **Adapting to Technological Advancements:** Embrace and adapt to technological advancements that impact the sales process. This could involve leveraging new sales tools, incorporating digital marketing strategies, or utilizing data analytics to gain insights into customer behaviour.

5. **Flexible Sales Pitches:** Develop flexible sales pitches that can be adapted to different customer needs and contexts. A one-size-fits-all approach is often ineffective; salespeople should be able to customize their pitch to address specific pain points and priorities of each customer.

6. **Responding to Customer Feedback:** Actively seek and respond to customer feedback. Adaptability involves a willingness to listen to customer perspectives, address concerns, and continuously refine products or services based on customer input.

7. **Navigating Economic Changes:** Stay attuned to economic changes that may impact customer spending behaviour. During economic shifts, salespeople should be adaptable in adjusting pricing strategies, offering flexible payment options, and positioning products or services as value-driven solutions.

8. **Learning from Setbacks:** View setbacks and challenges as learning opportunities. An adaptable salesperson learns from failures, adjusts strategies accordingly, and uses setbacks as stepping stones toward improvement.

9. **Cultural Sensitivity:** Demonstrate cultural sensitivity and adaptability when dealing with customers from diverse backgrounds. Understanding and respecting cultural nuances is crucial for building rapport and fostering positive relationships.

10. **Remote and Virtual Selling:** With the rise of remote work and virtual interactions, adaptability is essential for mastering the nuances of virtual selling. This includes utilizing video conferencing tools, optimizing online presentations, and adjusting to the unique challenges of virtual communication.

11. **Flexibility in Negotiations:** Exhibit flexibility in negotiations, recognizing that each customer may have different priorities and constraints. Being open to compromise and finding mutually beneficial solutions contributes to successful deal closures.

12. **Dynamic Problem-Solving:** Develop dynamic problem-solving skills. Adaptability involves the ability to think on one's feet, address unexpected challenges during sales interactions, and find creative solutions to meet customer needs.

13. **Staying Relevant with Training:** Invest in continuous learning and training to stay relevant in the industry. Adaptable salespeople proactively seek out opportunities to enhance their skills, whether through workshops, seminars, or online courses.

14. **Resilience in the Face of Rejection:** Cultivate resilience in the face of rejection. Adaptability involves bouncing back from setbacks, maintaining a positive mindset, and learning from rejection to improve future sales approaches.

15. **Building Long-Term Relationships:** Prioritize building long-term relationships with clients. An adaptable salesperson understands that customer needs may evolve over time, and maintaining flexibility in the relationship allows for ongoing collaboration and repeat business.

In summary, adaptability and flexibility are integral to a salesperson's success in a dynamic and competitive environment. By embracing change, adjusting strategies, and proactively responding to customer needs, sales professionals can build resilience, enhance customer relationships, and drive sustainable success in sales.

Compelling Storytelling

Compelling storytelling is a powerful tool for salespeople to engage customers, communicate value, and create memorable experiences. Here is a detailed summary of how a salesperson can effectively leverage compelling storytelling:

1. **Understanding Customer Needs:** Before crafting a story, a salesperson must thoroughly understand the needs, challenges, and aspirations of the customer. Tailoring the narrative to resonate with these specific elements enhances its relevance and impact.

2. **Establishing Emotional Connections:** Compelling storytelling goes beyond facts and figures; it taps into emotions. A salesperson should aim to create an emotional connection by crafting narratives that evoke empathy, understanding, or excitement.

3. **Identifying Unique Selling Points (USPs):** Storytelling is a vehicle to highlight the unique selling points (USPs) of a product or service. By weaving these key features into a narrative, a salesperson makes them more memorable and impactful for the customer.

4. **Building a Relatable Protagonist:** Every story needs a protagonist, and in the context of sales, the customer should

see themselves as the hero. Craft narratives where the customer is the protagonist, facing challenges that the product or service can help overcome.

5. **Structuring Stories Effectively:** Employ a well-structured narrative with a clear beginning, middle, and end. Introduce the customer to a situation or challenge, present the product or service as the solution, and conclude with the positive outcomes or benefits.

6. **Using Analogies and Metaphors:** Analogies and metaphors make complex concepts more accessible. Salespeople can use these literary devices to explain technical aspects, highlight benefits, or draw parallels between the customer's situation and successful outcomes.

7. **Incorporating Real-Life Examples:** Real-life examples and case studies add authenticity and credibility to the story. Sharing how the product or service has positively impacted others provides tangible evidence of its value.

8. **Showcasing Customer Testimonials:** Customer testimonials are compelling elements of storytelling. Integrate quotes or narratives from satisfied customers to reinforce the positive experiences others have had with the product or service.

9. **Adapting Stories to Various Audiences:** A skilled salesperson tailors their stories to different audiences. Whether presenting to executives, technical teams, or end-users, adapting the narrative to resonate with the specific concerns and interests of each group enhances its effectiveness.

10. **Creating Visual Narratives:** Enhance storytelling with visual elements such as charts, graphs, or multimedia presentations. Visual aids reinforce key points, make the narrative more engaging, and appeal to diverse learning preferences.

11. **Maintaining Authenticity:** Authenticity is crucial in storytelling. Salespeople should share genuine stories that align with the brand and product truthfully. Customers are more likely to connect with authentic narratives than those that feel overly scripted.

12. **Leveraging Personal Anecdotes:** When appropriate, incorporate personal anecdotes into the narrative. Sharing relatable stories from one's own experiences builds a personal connection with the customer and adds a human touch to the sales process.

13. **Encouraging Customer Participation:** Invite customers to be active participants in the story. Ask open-ended questions, encourage them to share their experiences, and weave their input into the ongoing narrative to create a collaborative storytelling experience.

14. **Utilizing the Power of Resolution:** Every compelling story has a resolution or climax. In a sales context, this is the moment when the customer visualizes the positive outcomes or solutions that the product or service provides. The resolution should leave a lasting impression.

15. **Follow-Up and Reinforcement:** After presenting a compelling story, follow up with reinforcement. Reiterate key points, provide additional information if needed, and continue to build on the narrative in subsequent interactions to reinforce the message.

In summary, compelling storytelling is an art that allows salespeople to communicate complex information in a memorable and impactful way. By understanding customer needs, building emotional connections, and weaving narratives that display product benefits, sales professionals can enhance customer engagement and increase the likelihood of successful sales outcomes.

Demonstration and Showmanship

Demonstration and showmanship are essential elements in the sales process, allowing salespeople to display the features, benefits, and unique aspects of a product or service in a captivating and memorable manner. Here is a detailed summary of how a salesperson can effectively leverage demonstration and showmanship:

1. **Understanding the Product:** Before conducting a demonstration, a salesperson must have a deep understanding of the product or service. Comprehensive product knowledge enables the salesperson to highlight key features, advantages, and use cases during the demonstration.

2. **Identifying Unique Selling Points (USPs):** Clearly identify the unique selling points of the product that differentiate it from competitors. Demonstrations should focus on displaying these distinctive features and how they address specific customer needs.

3. **Tailoring Demonstrations to Customer Needs:** Customize demonstrations to align with the specific needs and interests of the customer. Understanding the customer's pain points allows the salesperson to emphasize how the product or service provides solutions to their challenges.

4. **Creating Engaging Scripts:** Develop engaging scripts or narratives to accompany the demonstration. A well-crafted script ensures that the salesperson communicates key messages effectively, maintains the customer's attention, and guides them through the demonstration seamlessly.

5. **Utilizing Interactive Elements:** Incorporate interactive elements into the demonstration to actively engage the customer. This could involve hands-on participation, interactive displays, or the use of technology to enhance the customer's experience and involvement in the demonstration.

6. **Visual Aids and Multimedia:** Enhance the demonstration with visual aids and multimedia presentations. Visual elements such as videos, slides, or interactive presentations help convey information more effectively, making the demonstration visually appealing and impactful.

7. **Demonstrating Problem-Solving:** Frame the demonstration as a solution to the customer's challenges. Displaying how the product or service addresses specific problems reinforces its practicality and positions it as a valuable solution.

8. **Creating a Sense of Discovery:** Structure the demonstration to create a sense of discovery for the customer. Gradually unveil features and benefits, allowing the customer to uncover the value proposition organically, which can increase their sense of engagement and interest.

9. **Mastering Product Handling:** If applicable, master the art of product handling. A salesperson's ability to expertly handle the product or demonstrate its functions adds a level of professionalism and confidence, instilling trust in the customer.

10. **Storytelling within Demonstrations:** Weave storytelling into the demonstration to provide context and relatability. Sharing real-life examples or customer success stories enhances the narrative and illustrates the practical applications of the product.

11. **Showcasing Versatility:** Highlight the versatility of the product or service. Demonstrate how it can adapt to different scenarios, meet varied needs, or integrate seamlessly into the customer's existing processes. Versatility enhances the product's appeal.

12. **Focusing on Benefits, Not Just Features:** While features are important, the emphasis should be on the benefits the customer will gain. Clearly articulate how the features

translate into tangible advantages and improvements for the customer's specific situation.

13. **Utilizing the Power of Persuasion:** Apply persuasive techniques during the demonstration. This could involve emphasizing the urgency of the customer's needs, displaying the product's unique value proposition, or providing incentives to encourage immediate action.

14. **Handling Objections Proactively:** Anticipate potential objections and address them proactively during the demonstration. A skilled salesperson turns objections into opportunities to display how the product effectively overcomes challenges.

15. **Closing with Impact:** Conclude the demonstration with a compelling closing statement that reinforces the key benefits and encourages the customer to take the next steps. The closing should leave a lasting impression and prompt the customer to move forward in the sales process.

In summary, effective demonstration and showmanship in sales involve a combination of product knowledge, engagement strategies, and a customer-centric approach. By customizing demonstrations, creating engaging narratives, and displaying the practical applications of the product, salespeople can captivate customers, build confidence, and increase the likelihood of successful conversions.

Establishing Credibility

Establishing credibility is crucial for salespeople to gain the trust and confidence of potential customers. Here is a detailed summary of how a salesperson can effectively establish credibility:

1. **Expertise and Product Knowledge:** Possess in-depth knowledge about the product or service being offered. A credible salesperson demonstrates expertise, answering

questions accurately, and providing valuable insights that display a deep understanding of the industry.

2. **Continuous Learning:** Stay updated on industry trends, market changes, and advancements in the field. Credibility is reinforced when a salesperson can speak knowledgeably about the latest developments and demonstrate a commitment to ongoing learning.

3. **Professionalism and Presentation:** Project professionalism in appearance, communication, and conduct. A polished and well-presented image contributes to the perception of credibility, indicating a serious and competent approach to business.

4. **Client Success Stories:** Share success stories and testimonials from satisfied clients. Real-life examples provide tangible evidence of the salesperson's ability to deliver value and contribute to positive outcomes for customers.

5. **Transparent Communication:** Practice transparent and open communication. Credibility is enhanced when a salesperson is honest about product limitations, potential challenges, and any other relevant information. Transparency builds trust.

6. **Case Studies and Use Cases:** Develop comprehensive case studies and use cases that illustrate how the product or service has successfully addressed specific customer needs. These tangible examples demonstrate practical applications and reinforce credibility.

7. **Professional Certifications and Qualifications:** Highlight any relevant professional certifications or qualifications that enhance credibility. Certifications from recognized industry bodies or educational institutions add a level of legitimacy to the salesperson's expertise.

8. **Industry Involvement:** Actively participate in industry associations, events, and forums. Involvement in the industry community displays a commitment to staying connected, networking, and contributing to the broader professional ecosystem.

9. **Positive Online Presence:** Maintain a positive and professional online presence. This includes a well-crafted LinkedIn profile, positive reviews on professional platforms, and contributions to relevant online discussions. A strong online presence reinforces credibility.

10. **References and Referrals:** Offer references and encourage referrals from satisfied customers. Having clients who are willing to vouch for the salesperson's credibility provides prospective customers with firsthand accounts of successful collaborations.

11. **Admitting Limitations:** If the salesperson does not have an immediate answer, it is better to admit it and commit to finding the information rather than providing inaccurate or speculative responses. Honesty about limitations contributes to credibility.

12. **Building Long-Term Relationships:** Focus on building long-term relationships rather than prioritizing short-term gains. Credibility is cultivated over time through consistent delivery on promises, reliability, and a commitment to customer satisfaction.

13. **Understanding the Customer's Business:** Demonstrate a comprehensive understanding of the customer's business. By showing that the salesperson has taken the time to learn about the customer's industry, challenges, and goals, credibility is strengthened.

14. **Clear Communication of Value Proposition:** Clearly communicate the value proposition of the product or service. A credible salesperson can articulate how the offering solves

specific problems for the customer and adds measurable value to their operations.

15. **Tested and Proven Methods:** Highlight any tested and proven methods employed by the salesperson. This could include successful sales strategies, methodologies, or approaches that have consistently delivered positive results in similar situations.

In summary, establishing credibility as a salesperson requires a combination of expertise, professionalism, transparency, and a commitment to customer success. By displaying knowledge, providing evidence of past successes, and maintaining a trustworthy and ethical approach, a salesperson can build credibility and foster lasting relationships with clients.

Word of Mouth Marketing (WOMM)

Word of Mouth Marketing (WOMM) is a powerful and organic method of promoting products or services through customer recommendations and endorsements. Here is a detailed summary of how a salesperson can effectively leverage Word of Mouth Marketing:

1. **Delivering Exceptional Customer Experiences:** The foundation of Word-of-Mouth Marketing is exceptional customer experiences. A salesperson should prioritize customer satisfaction by delivering on promises, exceeding expectations, and providing outstanding service.

2. **Building Strong Relationships:** Foster strong and positive relationships with customers. When customers feel a personal connection with a salesperson, they are more likely to share their positive experiences with others, contributing to positive word of mouth.

3. **Active Listening and Understanding Needs:** Practice active listening to understand the unique needs and preferences of each customer. By addressing specific pain points and

customizing solutions, a salesperson increases the likelihood of customers sharing their positive experiences with others.

4. **Encouraging Customer Reviews and Testimonials:** Actively encourage customers to leave reviews and provide testimonials. Positive reviews on online platforms and testimonials on the company's website serve as valuable social proof and contribute to positive word of mouth.

5. **Leveraging social media:** Engage with customers on social media platforms. Share success stories, customer testimonials, and other positive interactions. Social media provides a wide-reaching platform for customers to share their experiences and recommendations.

6. **Creating Shareable Content:** Develop shareable content that customers find valuable. This could include informative articles, how-to guides, or visually appealing content that customers are inclined to share with their network, amplifying the reach of positive messages.

7. **Hosting Customer Referral Programs:** Implement customer referral programs that incentivize existing customers to refer new business. Rewarding customers for bringing in referrals not only encourages word of mouth but also creates a sense of loyalty and appreciation.

8. **Networking and Community Engagement:** Actively participate in networking events and community engagements. Building a positive presence within the community fosters word of mouth as customers discuss their experiences with a trusted salesperson.

9. **Providing Value Beyond Sales:** Go beyond the transaction by providing additional value. This could involve offering educational resources, helpful tips, or ongoing support. Customers who perceive value beyond the initial sale are more likely to become brand advocates.

10. **Responding Promptly to Feedback:** Pay close attention to customer feedback and respond promptly. Whether positive or negative, engaging with feedback shows a commitment to customer satisfaction and can turn negative experiences into positive ones.

11. **Highlighting Unique Selling Points:** Clearly communicate and highlight the unique selling points of the product or service. When customers understand and appreciate the distinctive aspects of what they have purchased, they are more likely to share these features with others.

12. **Showcasing Customer Success Stories:** Share customer success stories through various channels. This could involve featuring case studies on the company website, creating video testimonials, or displaying how customers have achieved positive outcomes using the product or service.

13. **Utilizing Influencer Collaborations:** Collaborate with influencers or thought leaders in the industry. Influencers can amplify positive messages about a product or service, reaching a broader audience and leveraging their credibility to enhance word of mouth.

14. **Engaging Employees as Brand Ambassadors:** Cultivate a culture where employees are brand ambassadors. When employees are enthusiastic about the products or services they represent, their positive experiences contribute to internal word of mouth, which can extend externally.

15. **Monitoring and Analysing Customer Sentiment:** Regularly monitor and analyse customer sentiment through feedback, reviews, and social media mentions. Understanding how customers perceive the brand allows a salesperson to proactively address concerns and capitalize on positive sentiments.

In summary, Word of Mouth Marketing is a result of exceptional customer experiences, strong relationships, and strategic efforts to encourage and amplify positive recommendations. By actively engaging with customers, leveraging online and offline channels, and fostering a culture of advocacy, a salesperson can harness the organic power of word of mouth to drive business growth and build a positive brand reputation.

Creating a Sence of Urgency

Creating a sense of urgency is a potent strategy for salespeople to prompt customers to take immediate action. Here is a detailed summary on how a salesperson can effectively create a sense of urgency:

1. **Highlighting Limited-Time Offers:** Communicate time-sensitive promotions, discounts, or special offers. Clearly convey that these deals are available for a limited time, compelling customers to act quickly to secure the benefits.

2. **Limited Inventory Messages:** Emphasize scarcity by communicating limited product availability. Messages such as "limited stock" or "while supplies last" instil a fear of missing out (FOMO) and drive customers to make quicker purchasing decisions.

3. **Countdowns and Timers:** Utilize countdowns and timers in marketing materials, websites, or promotional emails. A ticking clock visually reinforces the urgency and creates a psychological pressure for customers to decide promptly.

4. **Exclusive Early Access:** Offer exclusive early access to new products, services, or promotions for a limited time. This creates a sense of privilege for customers who act swiftly and can lead to increased engagement and faster decision-making.

5. **Limited-Time Pricing:** Introduce limited-time pricing or time-sensitive discounts. Clearly communicate that the discounted rates are applicable only for a short period,

motivating customers to make a purchase before prices increase.

6. **Seasonal or Event Tie-Ins:** Align urgency with specific seasons, holidays, or events. Creating promotions tied to a particular period, such as holiday sales or back-to-school offers, taps into the natural sense of urgency associated with these occasions.

7. **Highlighting Exclusivity:** Emphasize exclusivity by positioning a product or service as available to a select group or for a limited time. The perception of exclusivity enhances the perceived value and urgency associated with the offering.

8. **Limited-Edition Releases:** Introduce limited-edition or exclusive releases. Customers are often motivated to act quickly when they know that a product is only available for a short time, creating a sense of urgency to secure a unique item.

9. **Communicating Future Changes:** Alert customers to upcoming changes or updates. Whether it is a product redesign, pricing adjustments, or feature modifications, communicating that changes are on the horizon encourages customers to act before these alterations take place.

10. **Early-Bird Discounts:** Offer early-bird discounts for customers who commit to a purchase within a specified period. This incentivizes early decision-making and rewards customers who act swiftly.

11. **Limited-Time Trials or Samples:** Provide limited-time trials or samples. Allowing customers to experience a product or service for a short duration creates a time-bound opportunity for them to decide on a purchase.

12. **Immediate Benefits for Quick Action:** Clearly communicate the immediate benefits customers will receive by acting quickly. Whether it is instant access to a service,

quick delivery, or immediate cost savings, emphasizing immediate gratification enhances urgency.

13. **Personalized Urgency:** Implement personalized urgency based on customer behaviour. For example, sending targeted messages like "your exclusive offer expires soon" creates a personalized urgency tailored to individual customer interactions.

14. **Highlighting Demand:** Communicate high demand for the product or service. Messages such as "selling fast" or "highly sought after" create a fear of scarcity and encourage customers to make decisions promptly.

15. **Frequent, Consistent Communication:** Consistently communicate the urgency through various channels. Frequent reminders through emails, social media, and other communication channels reinforce the time-sensitive nature of the opportunity.

In summary, creating a sense of urgency involves strategically using time-sensitive elements, exclusivity, and incentives to motivate customers to take immediate action. By effectively conveying the urgency of an offer or opportunity, salespeople can drive quicker decision-making, capitalize on customer motivations, and ultimately boost sales and conversions.

B2B vs. B2C Marketing

Business-to-Business (B2B) marketing and Business-to-Consumer (B2C) marketing are distinct approaches, each tailored to the unique characteristics of their target audiences. Here is a detailed analysis of the differences between B2B and B2C marketing:

1. Target Audience:

- **B2B Marketing:** Targets other businesses or organizations. The decision-making process often involves multiple stakeholders, and the focus is on providing solutions that enhance efficiency, productivity, or profitability.

- **B2C Marketing:** Targets individual consumers. The decision-making process is typically more straightforward, often influenced by emotions, personal preferences, and immediate needs.

2. Purchase Process:

- **B2B Marketing:** Involves a more complex and longer sales cycle. Decision-making is often rational, fact-based, and may require consensus among a team of decision-makers.

- **B2C Marketing:** Generally, has a shorter sales cycle. Purchases are often impulsive, influenced by emotions, personal preferences, and individual needs.

3. Decision-Making Unit:

- **B2B Marketing:** Involves multiple decision-makers, including executives, managers, and possibly end-users. The purchase decision is often a collaborative effort.

- **B2C Marketing:** Typically involves an individual or a household making the purchase decision. The decision-maker is often the end-user of the product or service.

4. Relationship Building:

- **B2B Marketing:** Focuses on building long-term relationships. Relationship-building is crucial, as B2B transactions often involve ongoing contracts, partnerships, and repeated business.

- **B2C Marketing:** While relationship-building is important, the emphasis may be more on immediate transactions. Loyalty programs and customer engagement are used to encourage repeat business.

5. Marketing Channels:

- **B2B Marketing:** Relies heavily on personal selling, relationship management, content marketing, and industry events. Direct communication channels, such as email and professional networks, are often prioritized.

- **B2C Marketing:** Utilizes a broad range of channels, including mass media advertising, social media, influencers, and e-commerce platforms. B2C marketing often emphasizes reaching a large audience.

6. Content and Messaging:

- **B2B Marketing:** Content is usually more detailed, technical, and focused on demonstrating expertise. Messaging emphasizes how the product or service addresses business challenges and delivers measurable value.

- **B2C Marketing:** Content is often more visual, emotionally driven, and simplified. Messaging highlights the immediate benefits, emotions, and lifestyle enhancements associated with the product or service.

7. Pricing Structure:

- **B2B Marketing:** Involves complex pricing structures, often tailored to the specific needs and scale of the business. Negotiation and customization are common.

- **B2C Marketing:** Generally, has simpler and more transparent pricing structures. Discounts, promotions, and tiered pricing may be used to attract a wide range of consumers.

8. Branding and Positioning:

- **B2B Marketing:** Focuses on building a professional and trustworthy brand. Positioning is often centred around expertise, reliability, and the ability to deliver business solutions.

- **B2C Marketing:** Emphasizes building a brand that resonates with the lifestyle, values, and aspirations of the target consumer. Emotional branding is often a key component.

9. Customer Education:

- **B2B Marketing:** Involves detailed product or service education, often through webinars, whitepapers, and consultations. Buyers need to understand how the solution integrates into their business processes.

- **B2C Marketing:** While education is still important, it is generally more straightforward. Consumers want to know how a product or service benefits them personally and solves a specific problem.

10. Decision Triggers:

- **B2B Marketing:** Decision triggers are often based on rational considerations such as cost-effectiveness, efficiency gains, or strategic alignment.

- **B2C Marketing:** Decision triggers can be emotional, practical, or impulsive. They may be influenced by trends, social factors, or personal desires.

In summary, while both B2B and B2C marketing share fundamental principles, their strategies, tactics, and messaging must be tailored to the unique characteristics of their target audiences and the nature of the purchase decision. Understanding these differences is essential for developing effective marketing campaigns in each context.

So, B2B or B2C?

Deciding whether to market to Business-to-Business (B2B) or Business-to-Consumer (B2C) involves careful consideration of various factors that align with the nature of the product or service, target audience, and business goals. Here is a summary of key considerations for a salesperson when deciding between B2B and B2C marketing:

1. Product or Service Complexity:

- **B2B Marketing:** If the product or service is complex, involves customization, or addresses specific business needs, B2B marketing may be more appropriate. Businesses often require in-depth information and tailored solutions.

- **B2C Marketing:** For simpler and more straightforward products or services that cater to individual consumer needs, B2C marketing is suitable. The emphasis is often on ease of use and immediate benefits.

2. Target Audience:

- **B2B Marketing:** When the target audience comprises businesses, decision-makers, and professionals, B2B marketing is the logical choice. Understanding the needs and priorities of businesses is crucial for success.

- **B2C Marketing:** If the target audience is individual consumers with diverse preferences, lifestyles, and purchasing behaviours, B2C marketing is more appropriate. The focus is on reaching a broad consumer base.

3. Purchase Decision Process:

- **B2B Marketing:** Consider the length and complexity of the decision-making process. If sales involve negotiations, consultations, and consensus-building among multiple stakeholders, B2B marketing is likely the better fit.

- **B2C Marketing:** If the decision-making process is relatively quick, emotional, and involves individual preferences, B2C marketing aligns with the more straightforward consumer purchasing journey.

4. Relationship Building:

- **B2B Marketing:** If building long-term relationships with businesses and fostering ongoing partnerships is a priority,

B2B marketing is suitable. B2B transactions often involve repeated business and collaborative ventures.

- **B2C Marketing:** While relationship-building is essential, the emphasis may be more on immediate transactions and creating positive brand associations to encourage repeat purchases.

5. Scale and Volume:

- **B2B Marketing:** Assess the scale of potential clients and transactions. B2B marketing often involves fewer, high-value transactions. Success may be measured in terms of quality relationships and strategic partnerships.

- **B2C Marketing:** If the business model is built on reaching a large volume of individual consumers with lower-value transactions, B2C marketing is the preferred approach.

6. Brand Positioning:

- **B2B Marketing:** Focus on building a professional and trustworthy brand. Positioning should emphasize expertise, reliability, and the ability to deliver tailored business solutions.

- **B2C Marketing:** Emphasize building a brand that resonates with the lifestyle, values, and aspirations of individual consumers. Emotional branding and relatable messaging are often key components.

7. Marketing Channels:

- **B2B Marketing:** Leverage channels that reach businesses, such as professional networks, industry events, and targeted email campaigns. Personal selling and relationship management are crucial components.

- **B2C Marketing:** Utilize a diverse range of channels, including mass media advertising, social media, influencers, and e-commerce platforms, to reach a broad consumer audience.

8. Industry and Market Trends:

- **B2B Marketing:** Consider industry-specific trends and market dynamics. B2B marketing strategies may need to align with the unique challenges and opportunities within the targeted business sector.

- **B2C Marketing:** Assess trends in consumer behaviour, preferences, and market demands. B2C marketing should be adaptable to changes in consumer expectations and emerging trends.

9. Customer Communication Preferences:

- **B2B Marketing:** Recognize that businesses may prefer in-depth communication, detailed presentations, and consultations. Building relationships often involves direct and personalized communication.

- **B2C Marketing:** Understand that consumers often prefer concise, visually appealing content, and may respond well to emotionally driven storytelling. Engaging and relatable communication is crucial.

10. Financial Considerations:

- **B2B Marketing:** Recognize that B2B transactions may involve larger deal sizes but longer sales cycles. Consider the financial resources required for sustained relationship-building and tailored solutions.

- **B2C Marketing:** Acknowledge that B2C transactions may involve smaller deal sizes but higher transaction volumes. Consider the financial resources needed for mass marketing, branding, and customer acquisition.

In summary, the decision to market to B2B or B2C depends on a thorough analysis of the product or service, the target audience, the sales process, and overall business objectives. Tailoring marketing strategies to align with the unique characteristics of the chosen market segment is essential for success.

How would Jake Sanderson identify his target market?

Let us consider Jake Sanderson, the creative salesperson selling sand products designed for building durable and creative sandcastles. Jake can weigh several factors to determine whether to incorporate Business-to-Business (B2B) or Business-to-Consumer (B2C) marketing for his sand products:

1. **Product Characteristics:**

   - If Jake's sand products are designed for large-scale projects, such as landscaping or construction, B2B marketing might be suitable. For example, selling to resorts, amusement parks, or construction companies.

   - If the sand products are more tailored for individual use, such as home sandboxes or beach enthusiasts, B2C marketing could be the better fit.

2. **Target Audience:**

   - B2B Marketing: Jake should assess whether businesses or institutions are the primary consumers. If his target audience includes resorts, construction companies, or landscape architects, B2B marketing is appropriate.

   - B2C Marketing: If Jake's sand products are meant for individual consumers, families, or hobbyists, B2C marketing aligns with reaching a broader consumer base.

3. **Purchase Decision Process:**

   - B2B Marketing: Consider the complexity of the decision-making process. If Jake's sand products require negotiations, consultations, and approval from multiple stakeholders, B2B marketing is likely suitable.

- B2C Marketing: If the decision-making process is more straightforward and influenced by individual preferences, emotions, and immediate needs, B2C marketing is a better choice.

4. **Relationship Building:**

- B2B Marketing: If building long-term relationships with businesses and fostering partnerships is a priority for Jake, B2B marketing is the way to go. This may involve tailored solutions, ongoing contracts, and collaboration.

- B2C Marketing: If the emphasis is on immediate transactions and creating positive brand associations to encourage repeat purchases, B2C marketing is more suitable.

5. **Scale and Volume:**

- B2B Marketing: If Jake anticipates selling larger quantities to a smaller number of clients, B2B marketing aligns with the business model. Deals may be of higher value, and relationships may be more personalized.

- B2C Marketing: If Jake's business model involves reaching a large volume of individual consumers with lower-value transactions, B2C marketing is more appropriate.

6. **Brand Positioning:**

- B2B Marketing: If Jake wants to position his brand as a professional and reliable supplier for businesses, B2B marketing allows him to emphasize expertise, reliability, and tailored business solutions.

- B2C Marketing: If the focus is on building a brand that resonates with the lifestyle and creativity of individual consumers, B2C marketing emphasizes emotional branding and relatable messaging.

7. **Marketing Channels:**

- B2B Marketing: If Jake aims to reach businesses, professional networks, industry events, and targeted email campaigns could be effective marketing channels. Personal selling and relationship management are crucial components.

- B2C Marketing: If reaching a broad consumer audience is the goal, Jake can utilize mass media advertising, social media, influencers, and e-commerce platforms.

8. **Industry and Market Trends:**

- B2B Marketing: Jake should consider industry-specific trends and market dynamics. B2B marketing strategies may need to align with the unique challenges and opportunities within the commercial construction or landscaping sectors.

- B2C Marketing: Jake needs to stay abreast of trends in consumer behaviour, preferences, and market demands to adapt his B2C marketing strategies accordingly.

Ultimately, Jake's decision should be informed by a thorough analysis of these factors and a clear understanding of his business goals. He may also consider a hybrid approach, incorporating elements of both B2B and B2C marketing based on the diverse applications of his sand products.

5 Years Later...

Five years had woven their golden threads into the tapestry of Jake Sanderson's sand-filled journey. What began as a lone crusade to sell sand on a beach had evolved into a flourishing empire of creativity and commerce.

Jake's company, aptly named "SandSculpt Solutions," had become synonymous with innovation, capturing the essence of both B2B and B2C markets. Nestled along the coast, the headquarters stood as a beacon of success, overlooking the very sands that birthed the WetWonder and the DryDream.

The WetWonder, once a quirky idea in Jake's mind, had become the darling of landscaping companies across the nation. Its unique moisture-retaining properties proved a game-changer, transforming arid landscapes into lush paradises. Business partnerships flourished, with SandSculpt Solutions becoming a go-to supplier for commercial ventures seeking sustainable solutions.

On the flip side, the DryDream had become a staple for families, beach resorts, and the young-at-heart. The beachgoers dream of creating intricate sandcastles that defied the tide found its vessel in the DryDream. Its popularity surged, and Jake found himself shipping containers of his magical sand to various corners of the globe.

As the company prospered, so did its team. What started as a one-man show had blossomed into a diverse ensemble of creative minds, each contributing to the ever-expanding repertoire of SandSculpt Solutions. The laughter echoing through the office was a testament to not just professional success, but a workplace filled with camaraderie and shared dreams.

Jake, the maestro of this sand-filled symphony, often found himself reminiscing about that first day on the beach. With each passing tide, the footprints he left had multiplied, forming a legacy etched in the sands of time. The local community thrived, thanks to job opportunities and partnerships that Jake had forged with neighbouring businesses.

As the sun dipped below the horizon, casting a warm glow on the sandcastle-filled beaches, Jake couldn't help but smile. His once improbable venture had become a tale of inspiration—a story told in grains of sand, shaping dreams, and turning them into castles…

Epilogue: "Sands of Success: A Whimsical Journey in Sales"

Dear Readers,

As we reach the final grains of this whimsical adventure in the world of sales, let us pause and build a sandcastle of reflection together. Our protagonist, Jake Sanderson, has shown us that selling sand on a beach is not only possible but can be an art form. In the dance of commerce, Jake pirouetted through the challenges, leaving a trail of sandy success behind.

In this tale of business ballet, we explored the delicate art of selling sand to businesses (B2B) and individuals (B2C). Whether the stage was set for a grand production with corporate partners or an intimate gathering with individual enthusiasts, Jake's every move was a choreography of connection.

Picture this: the sun dipping below the horizon, casting hues of amber and coral on the sandy canvas. The waves, like the ebb and flow of market trends, caressed the shore. Jake stood, a silhouette against the sunset, armed not with a sword, but with the knowledge of market intricacies and the art of persuasion.

In the symphony of sales, Jake composed his pitch, harmonizing the intricacies of B2B and B2C marketing. He swirled the wet and dry sands of his product's unique selling points, shaping them into castles that withstood the tide of scepticism.

As we close this chapter, let us take a moment to build our own sandcastle of wisdom:

- **Know Your Audience:** Just as Jake discerned between businesses and consumers, understanding your audience is the foundation of a sturdy castle.

- **Dance with Complexity:** Whether the waltz of B2B or the tango of B2C, the dance of sales can be intricate. Embrace the complexity and let it lead you to success.

- **Craft Relationships Like Sand Sculptures:** Jake understood that relationships are the building blocks of enduring success. Sculpt your connections with care and watch them withstand the test of time.

- **Ride the Waves of Change:** Markets, like the ocean, are ever-changing. Be the surfer who rides the waves, adapting and thriving with each new tide.

- **Leave Footprints of Value:** Just as Jake left footprints in the sand, leave footprints of value in the hearts of your customers. Let them remember the joy of building something extraordinary with your product.

As the sun bids adieu and the waves whisper their secrets, remember the magic of sand. It is not just a grain; it is a story waiting to be told, a castle waiting to be built. So, dear readers, go forth, armed with the knowledge from these sandy pages. Build your castles, dance your dances, and may your journey in sales be as enchanting as a day at the beach.

With sandy wishes and a pocketful of dreams,

Keith Kirby
Author of *"How to: Sell Sand on a Beach!"*